HAVE YOU
SEEN THIS
WIZARD?

AZKABAN PRISON

APPROACH WITH EXTREME CAUTION

BIG NOTE PIANO

Music by **John Williams**
Patrick Doyle &
Nicholas Hooper

Arranged by
Carol Matz

Alfred

Copyright © MMIX by Alfred Publishing Co., Inc.
All Rights Reserved. Printed in USA.
ISBN-10: 0-7390-6047-3
ISBN-13: 978-0-7390-6047-6

HARRY'S WONDROUS WORLD

By **JOHN WILLIAMS**
Arranged by Carol Matz

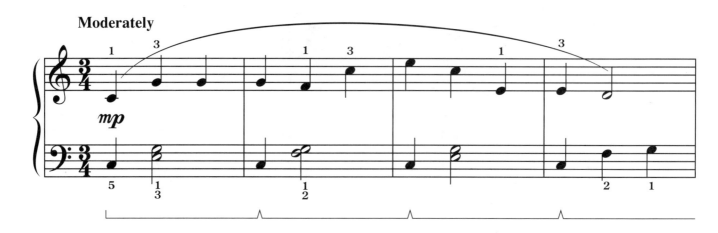

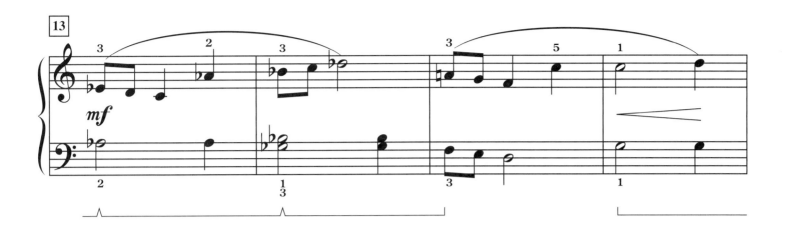

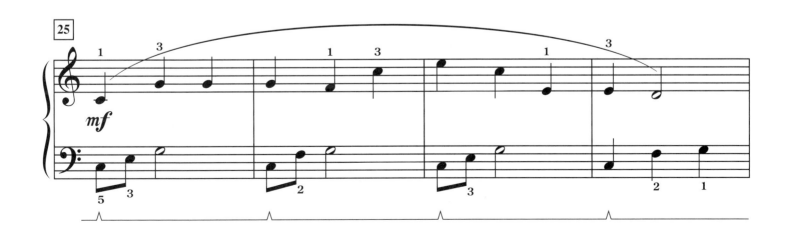

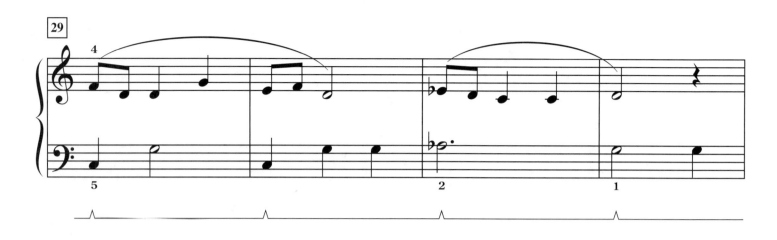

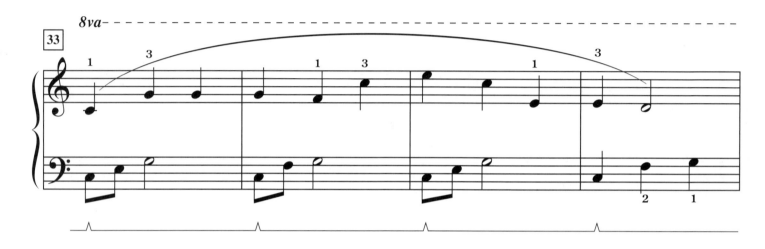

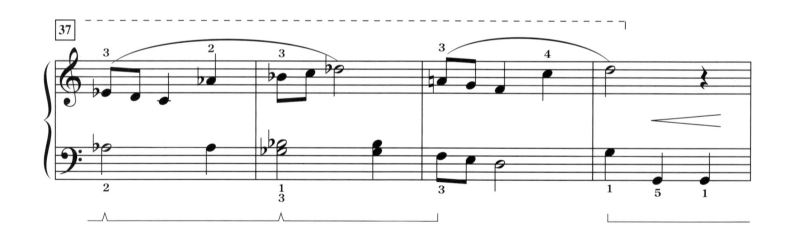

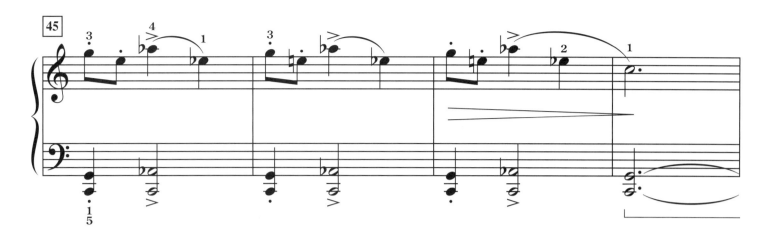

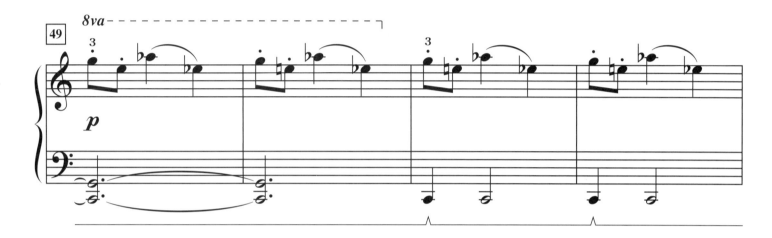

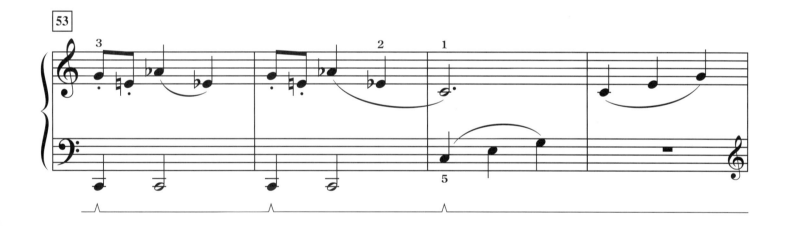

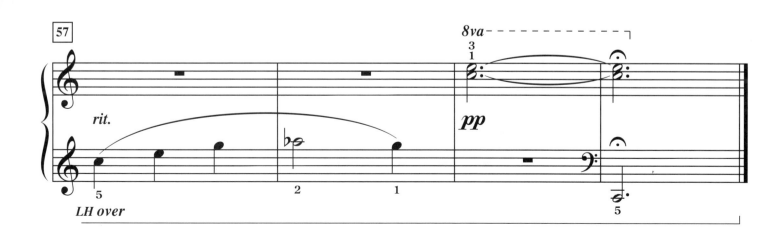

HEDWIG'S THEME

By **JOHN WILLIAMS**
Arranged by Carol Matz

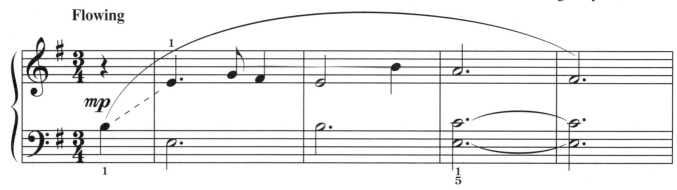

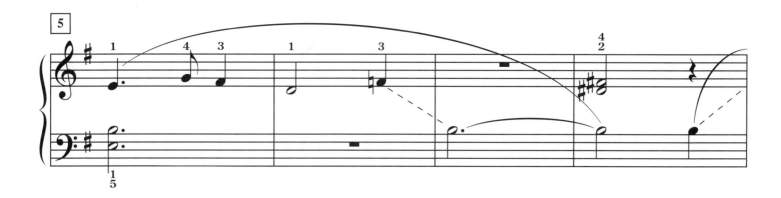

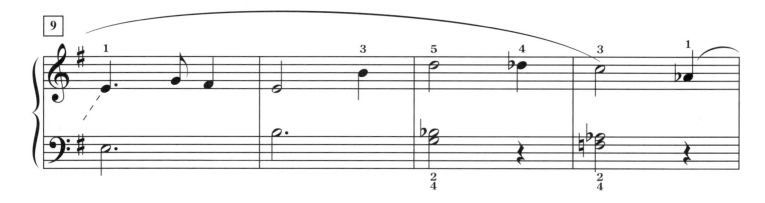

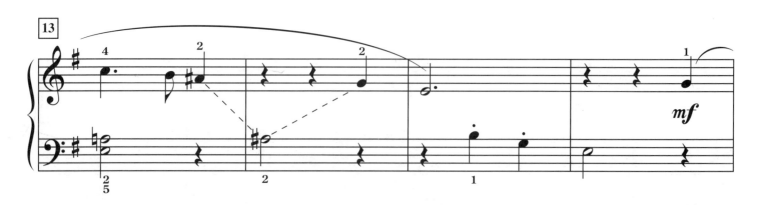

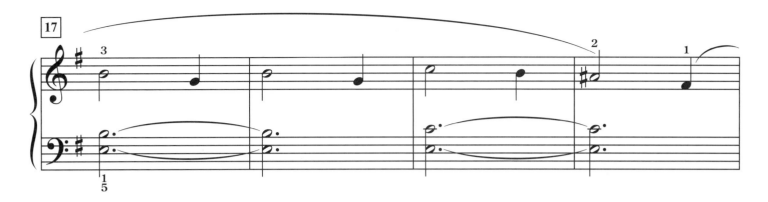

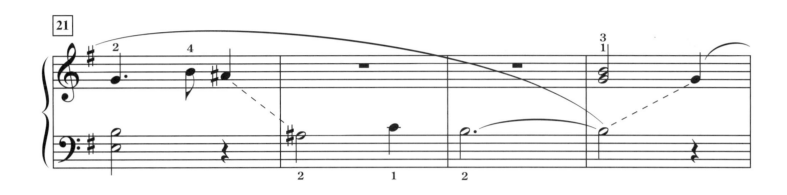

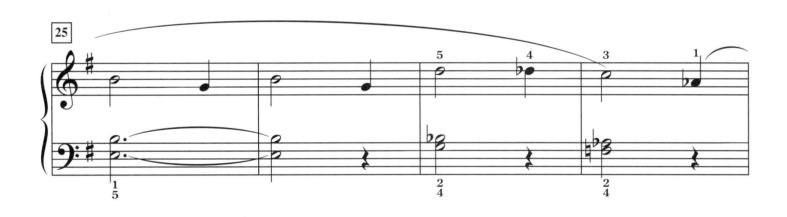

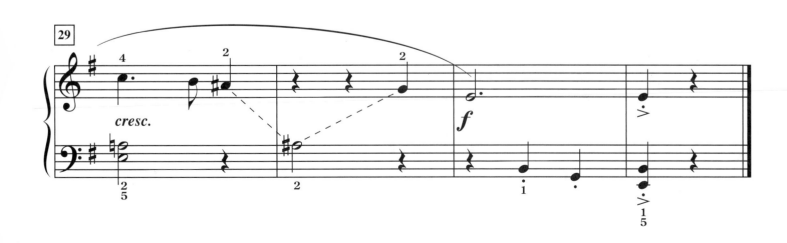

NIMBUS 2000

By **JOHN WILLIAMS**
Arranged by Carol Matz

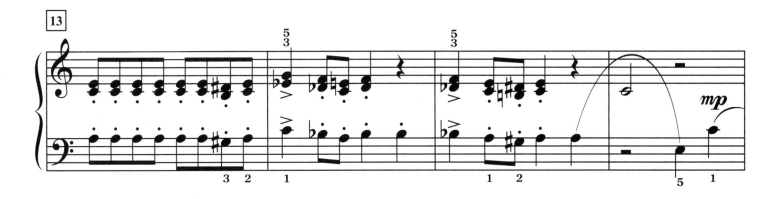

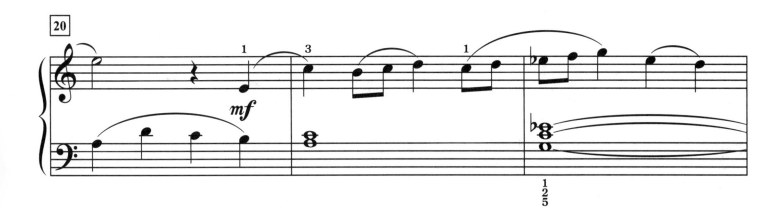

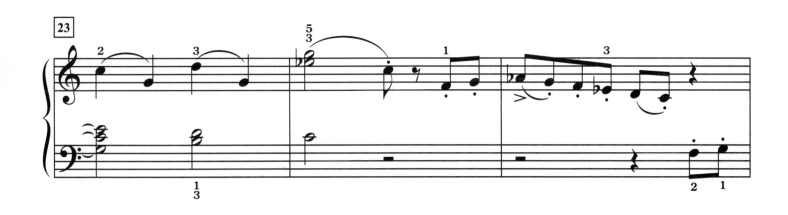

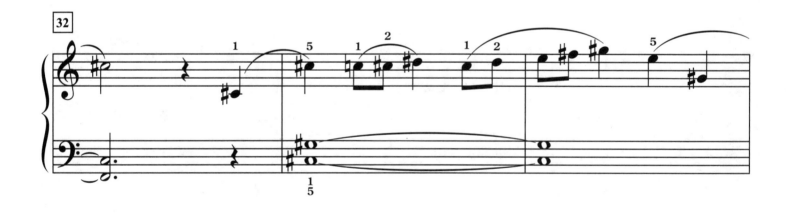

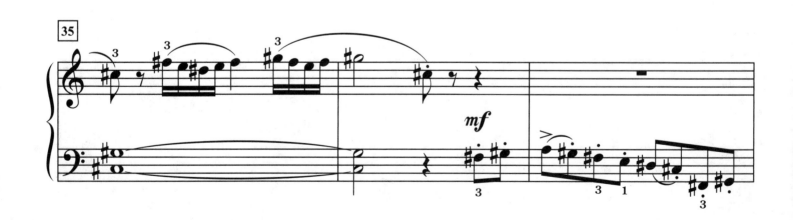

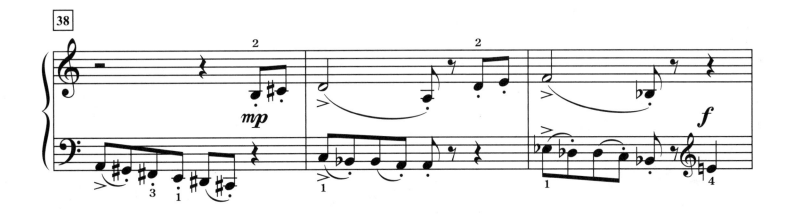

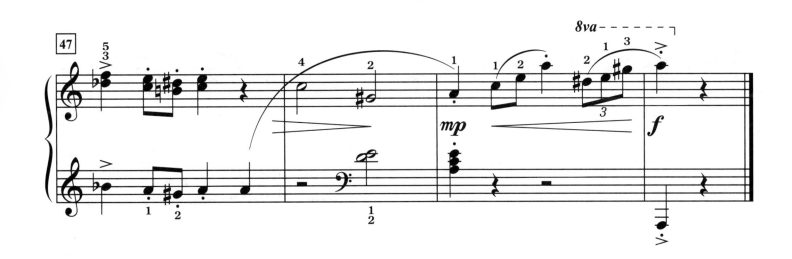

FAWKES THE PHOENIX

By **JOHN WILLIAMS**
Arranged by Carol Matz

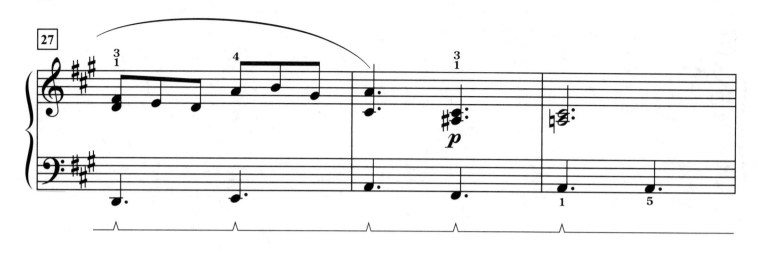

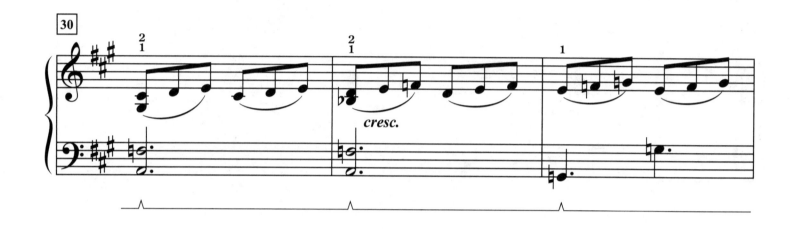

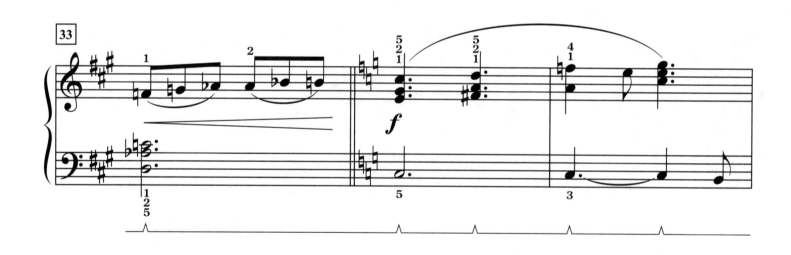

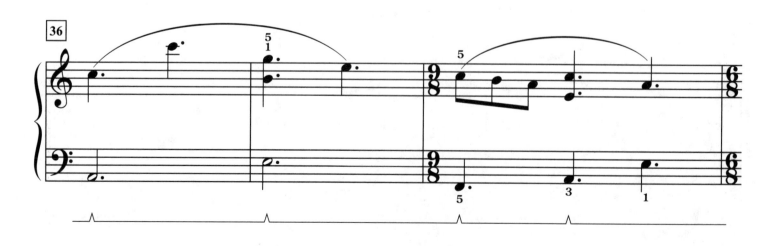

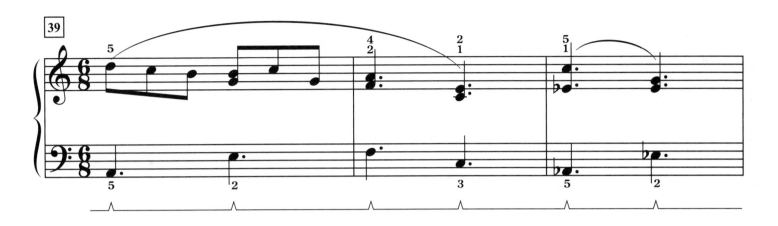

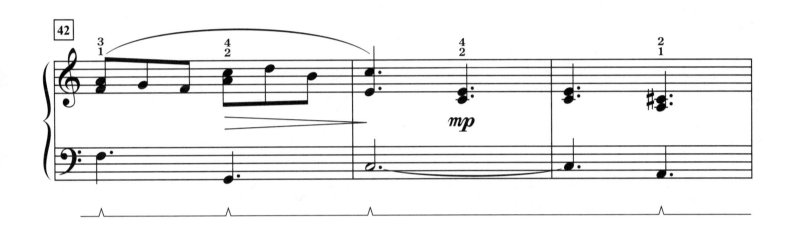

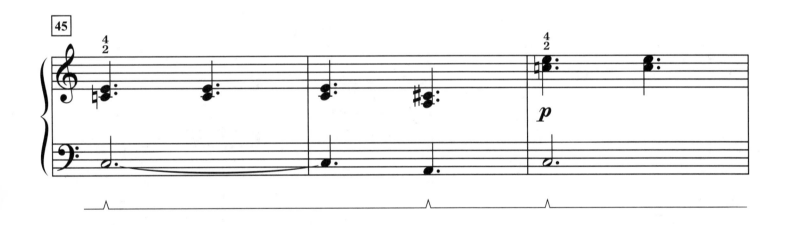

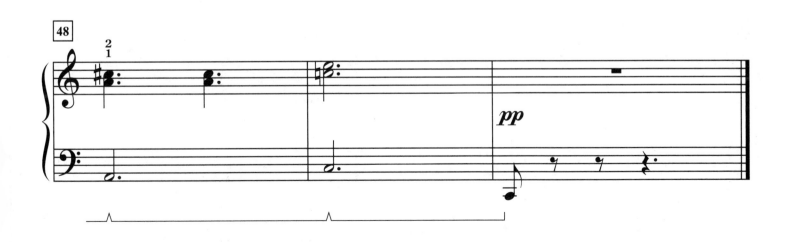

MOANING MYRTLE

Music by **JOHN WILLIAMS**
Arranged by Carol Matz

DOUBLE TROUBLE

By **JOHN WILLIAMS**
Arranged by Carol Matz

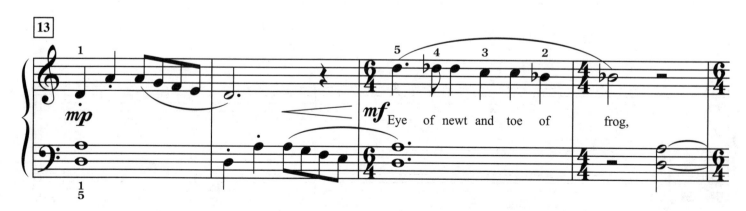

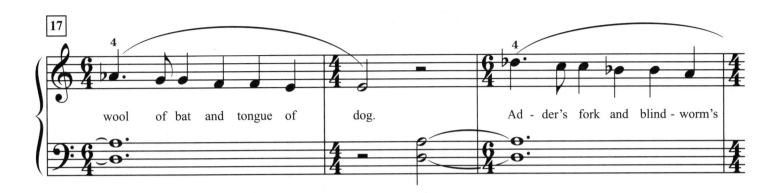

wool   of bat and tongue of   dog.   Ad - der's fork and blind - worm's

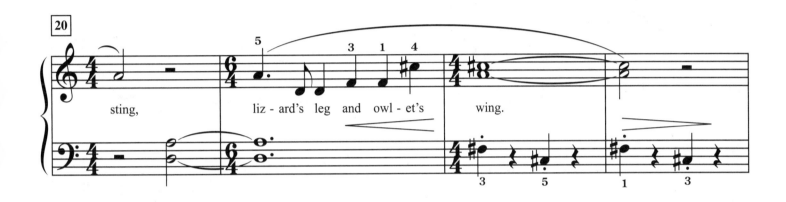

sting,   liz - ard's leg and owl - et's   wing.

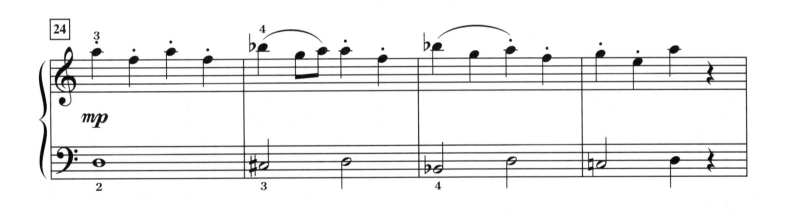

Dou - ble, dou - ble   toil and trou - ble;   fire____ burn and   caul - dron bub - ble.

HAGRID THE PROFESSOR

By **JOHN WILLIAMS**
Arranged by Carol Matz

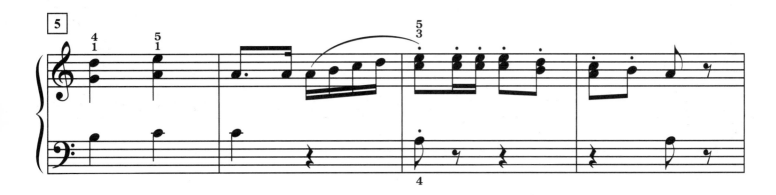

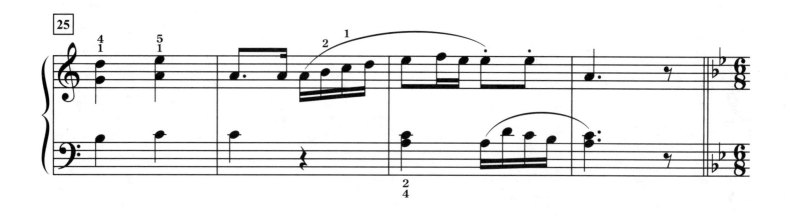

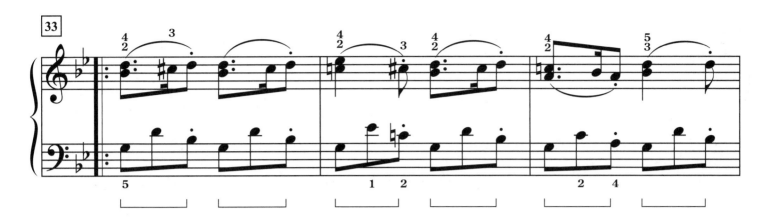

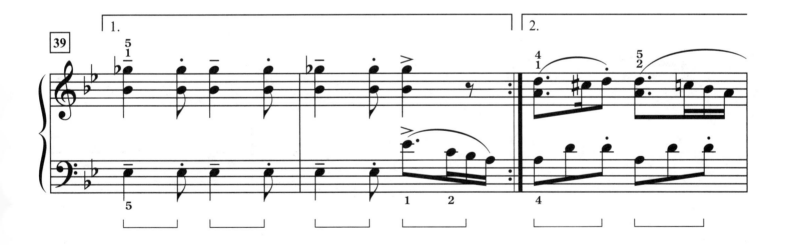

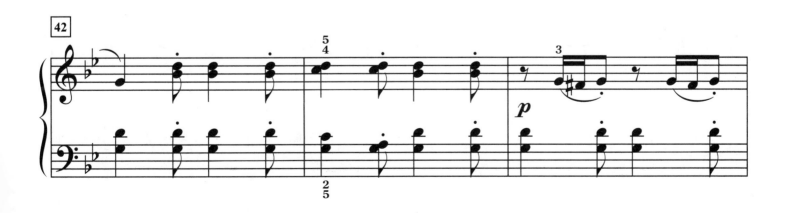

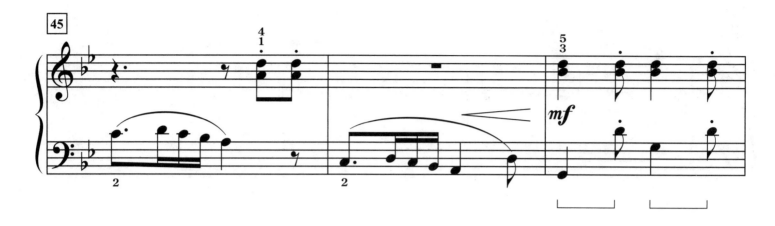

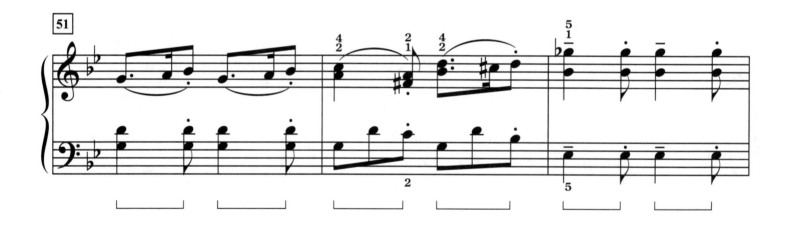

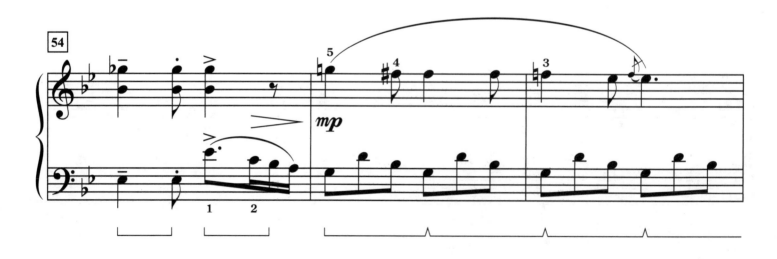

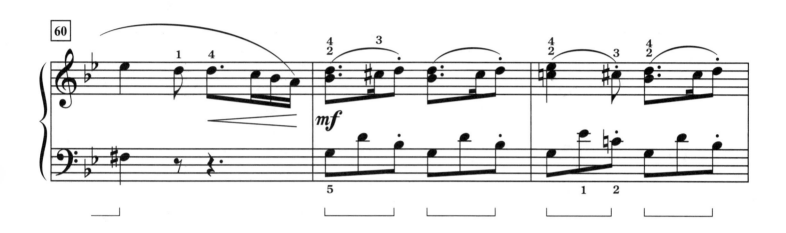

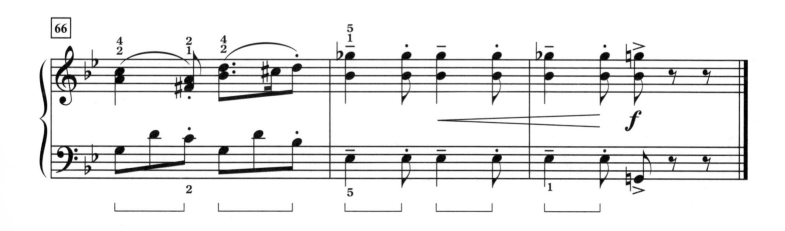

HARRY IN WINTER

By Patrick Doyle
Arranged by Carol Matz

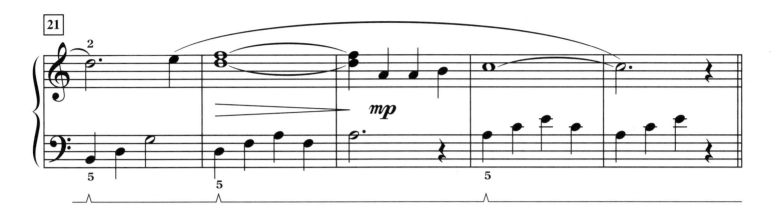

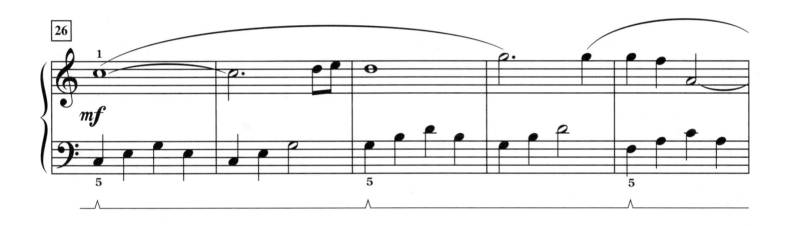

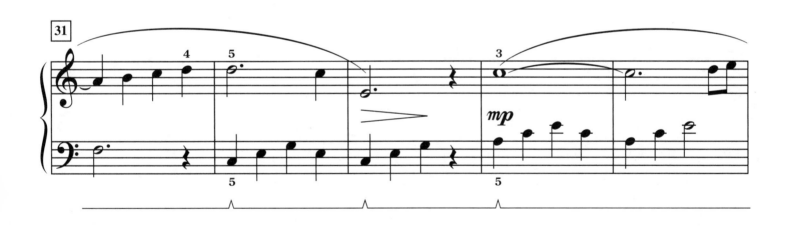

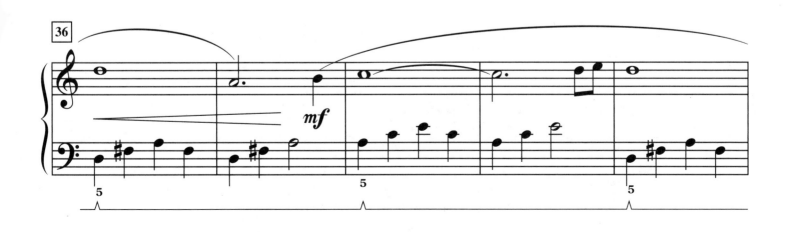

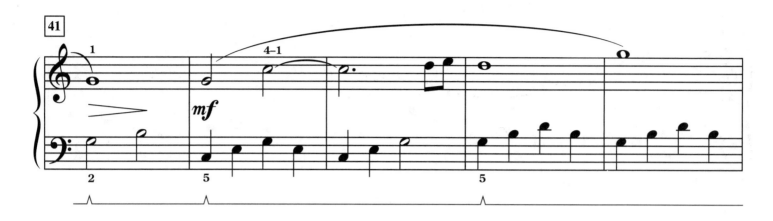

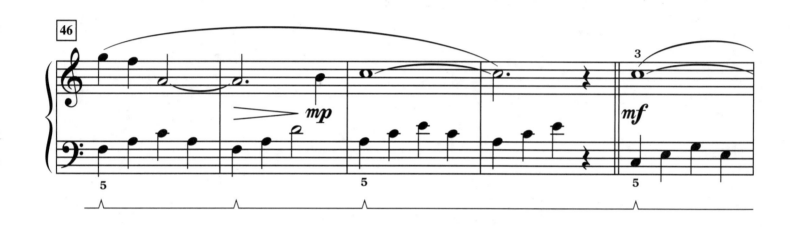

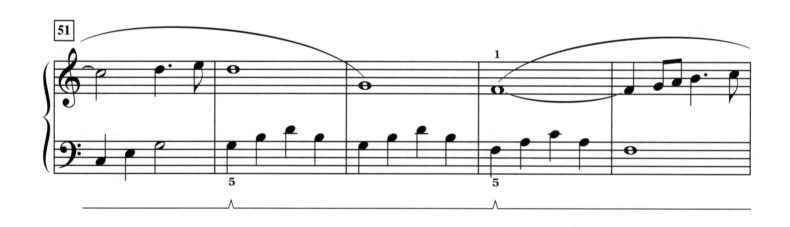

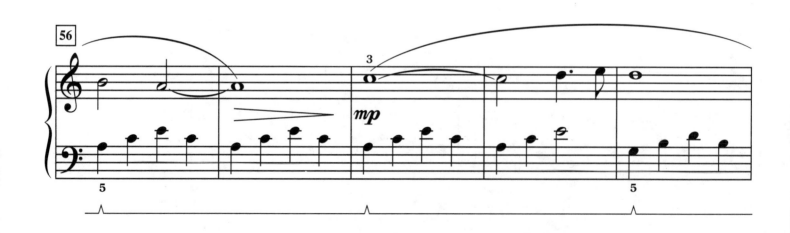

HOGWARTS' HYMN

By Patrick Doyle
Arranged by Carol Matz

Slowly, expressively

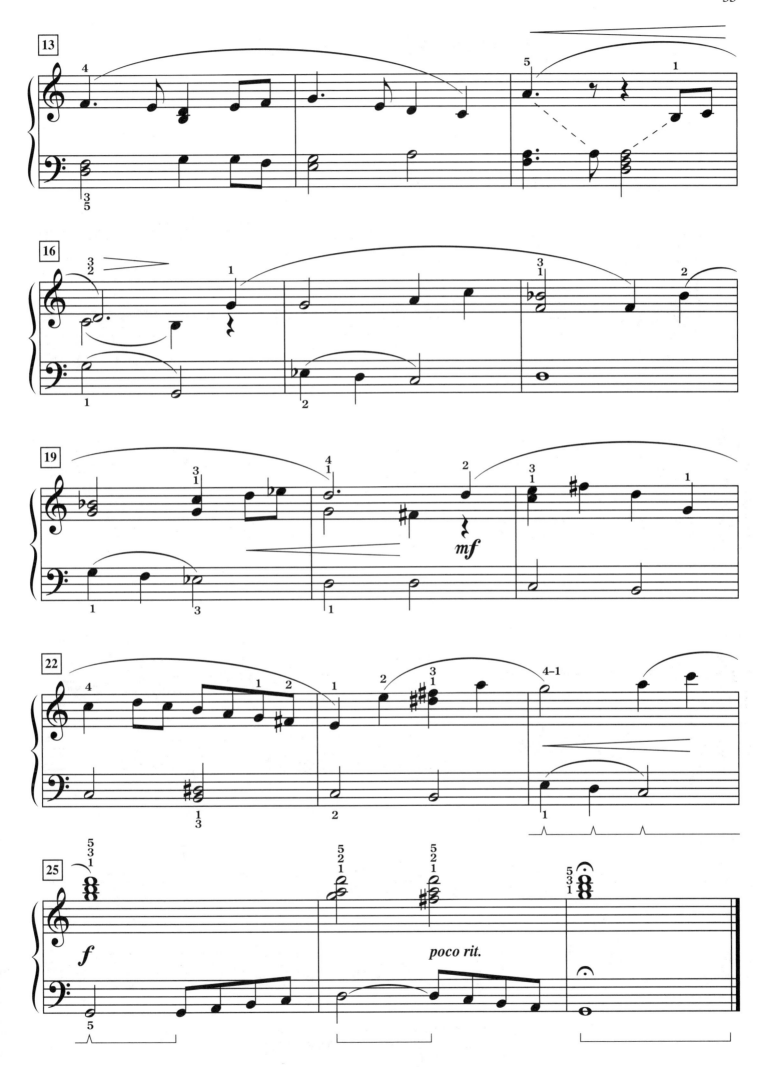

HOGWARTS' MARCH

By Patrick Doyle
Arranged by Carol Matz

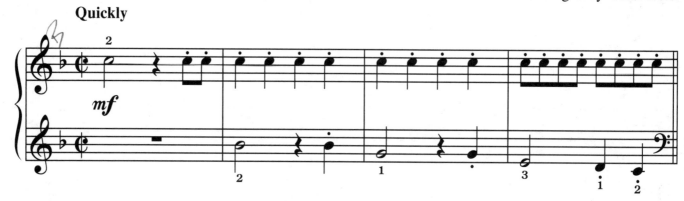

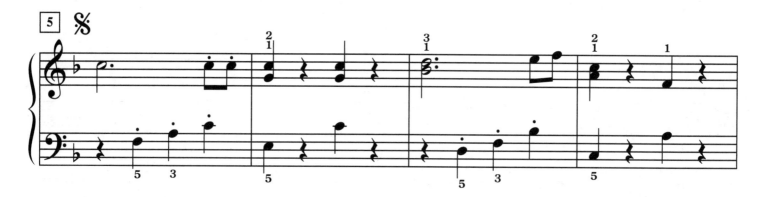

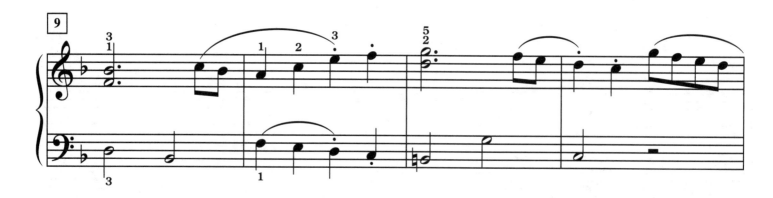

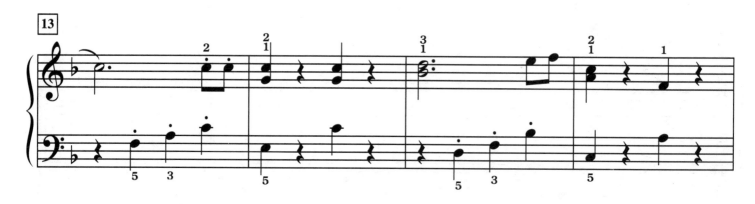

POTTER WALTZ

By Patrick Doyle
Arranged by Carol Matz

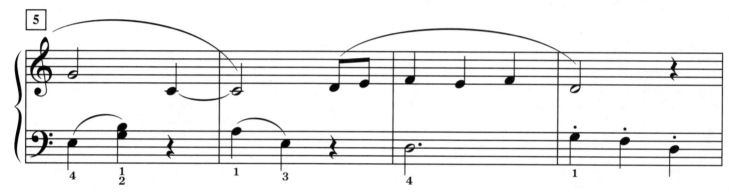

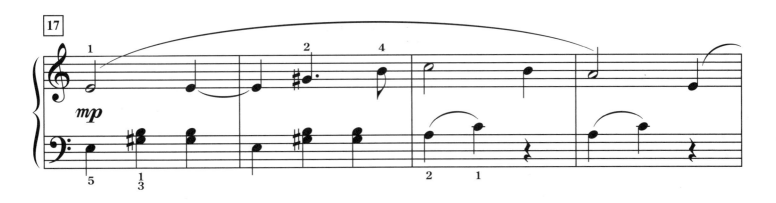

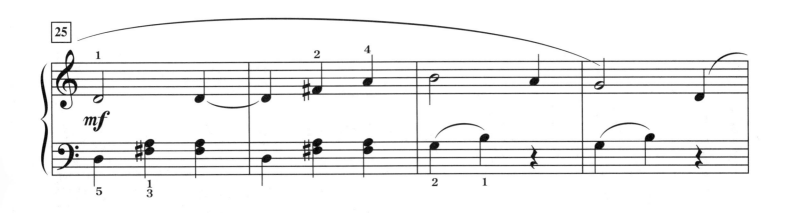

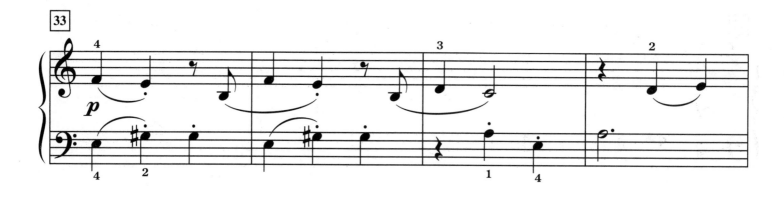

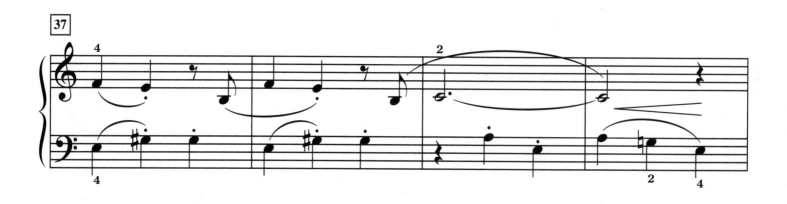

THE QUIDDITCH WORLD CUP

(The Irish)

By Patrick Doyle
Arranged by Carol Matz

Fast Irish jig

DUMBLEDORE'S ARMY

(Patronus)

By Nicholas Hooper
Arranged by Carol Matz

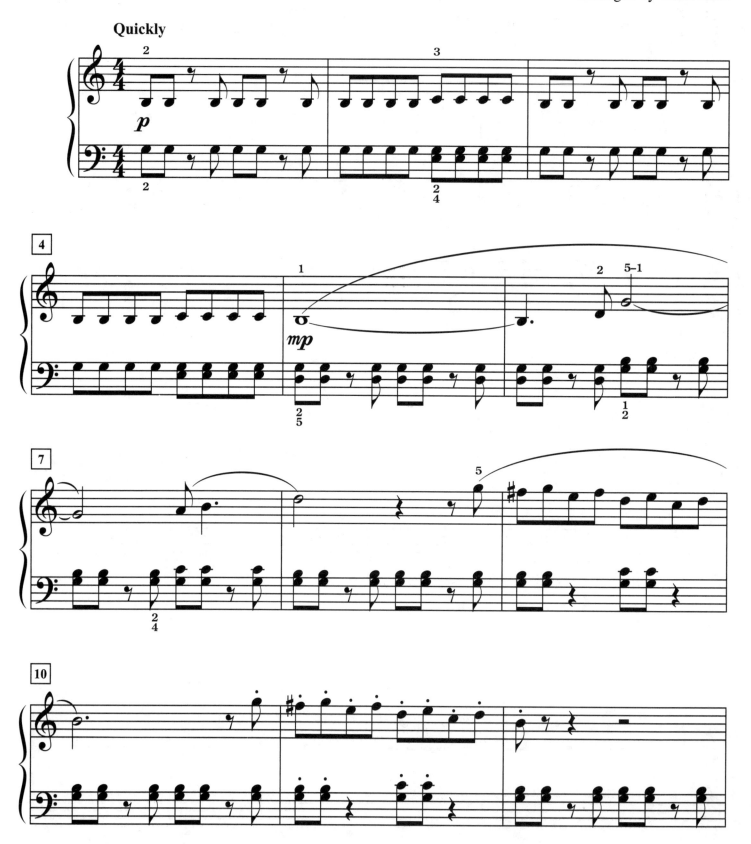

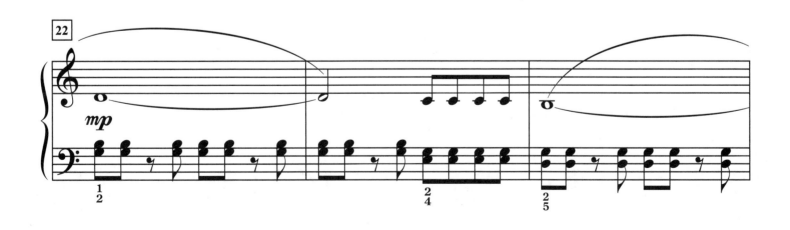

FIREWORKS

By Nicholas Hooper
Arranged by Carol Matz

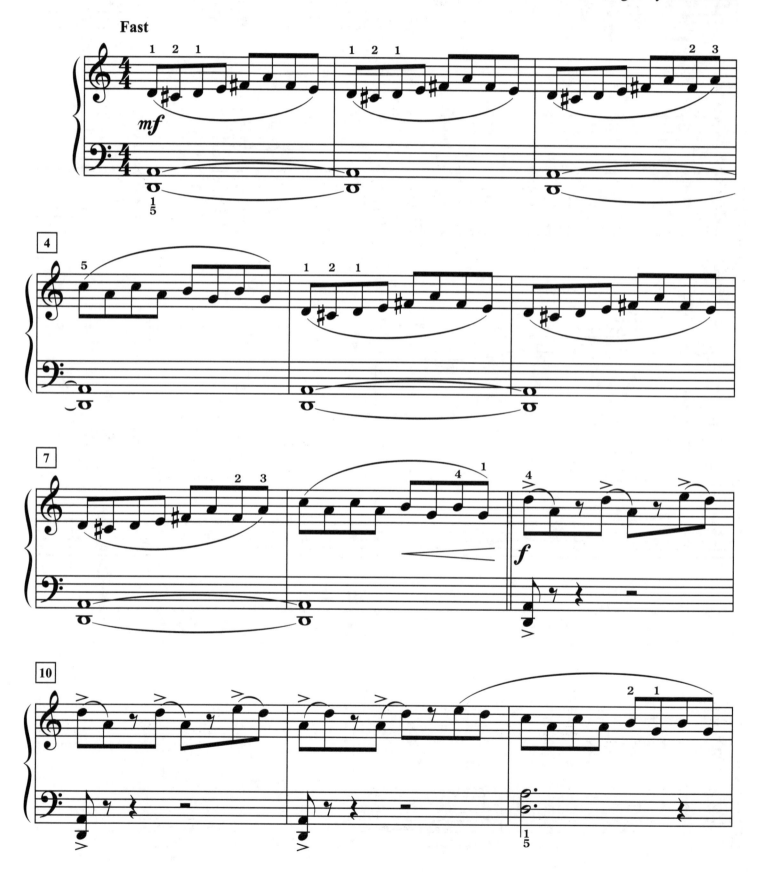

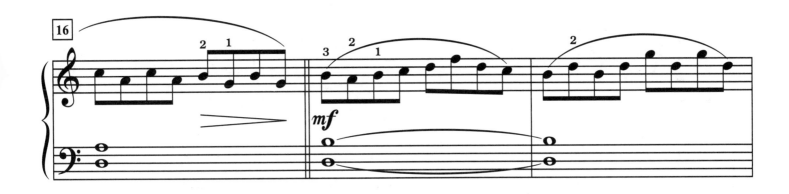

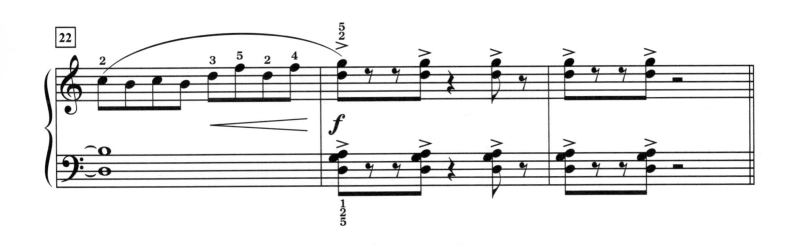

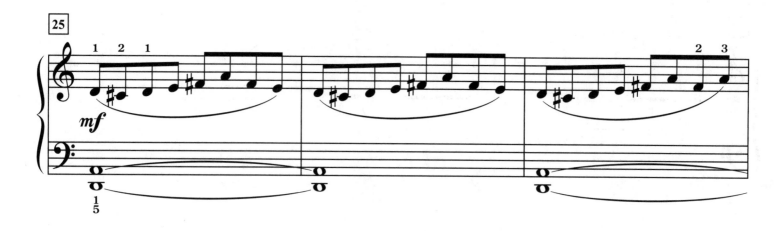

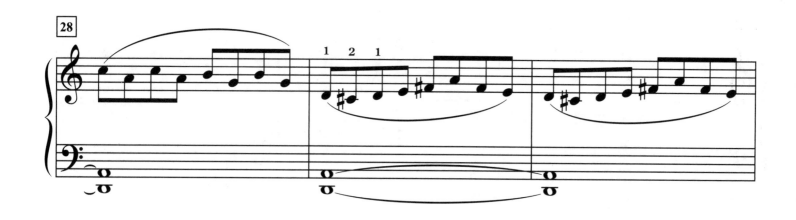

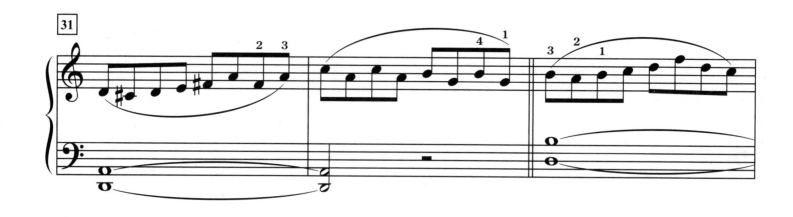

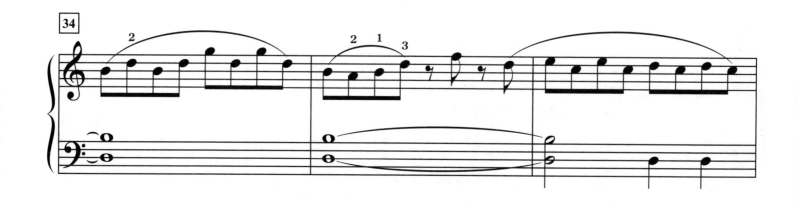

THE ROOM OF REQUIREMENT

By Nicholas Hooper
Arranged by Carol Matz

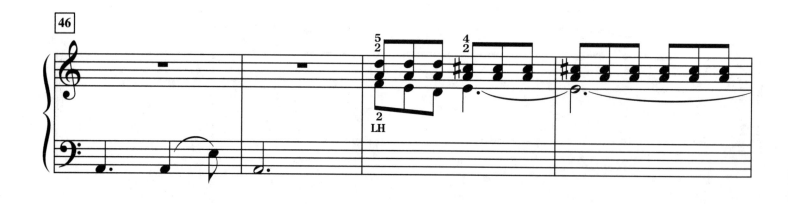

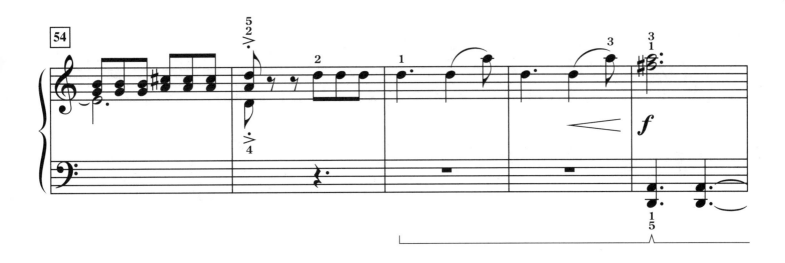

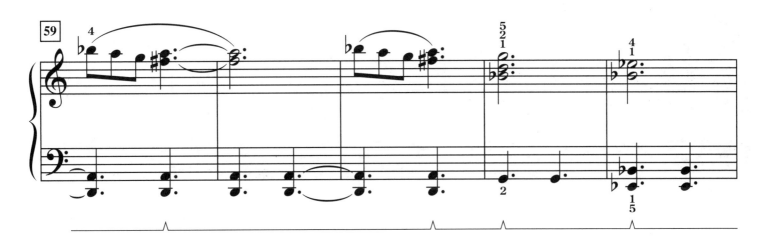

PROFESSOR UMBRIDGE

By Nicholas Hooper
Arranged by Carol Matz

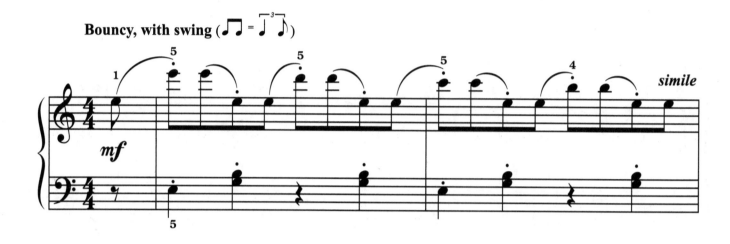

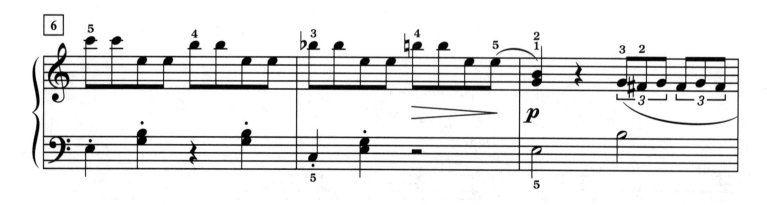

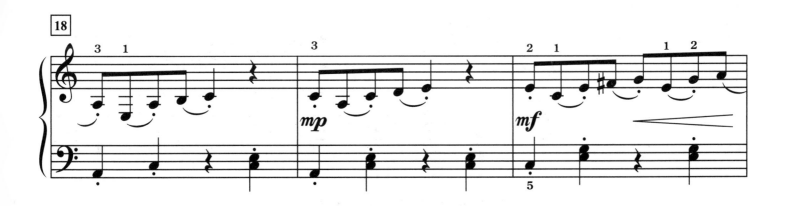

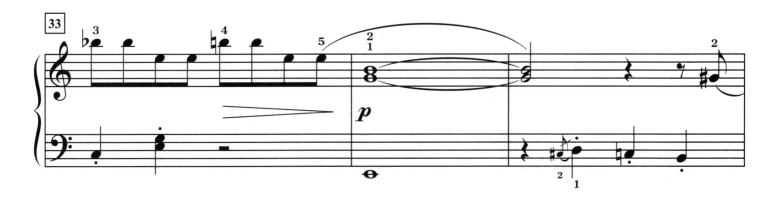

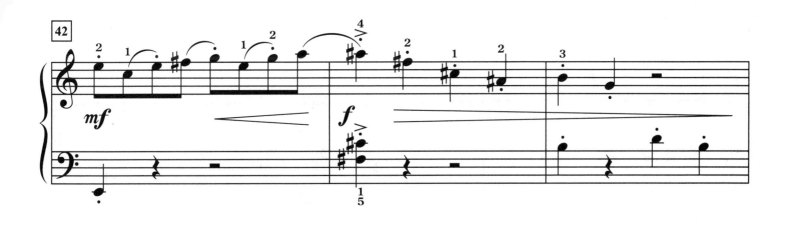

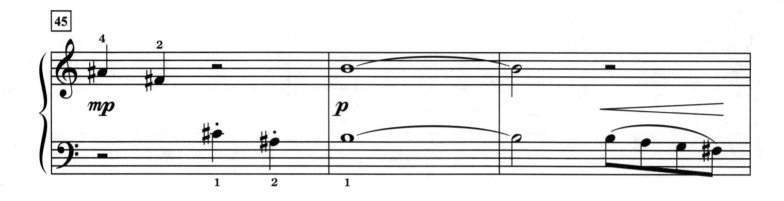

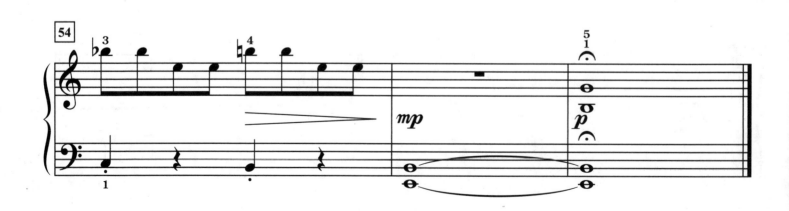